Finding Jesus After My Storm

Stephanie Defrance Williams

Copyright © 2021 by Stephanie Defrance Williams

All rights reserved. No part of this publication may be reproduced, distributed or transmitted in any form or by any means, including photocopying, recording, or other electronic or mechanical methods, without the prior written permission of the publisher, except in the case of brief quotations embodied in critical reviews and certain other noncommercial uses permitted by copyright law. For mission requests, write to the publisher, addressed " Attention: Permissions Coordinator," at the address below.

Stephanie Defrance Williams/Rejoice Essential Publishing

PO BOX 512

Effingham, SC 29541

www.republishing.org

Author Photo Credit: Heidihutayanaphoto.com

Unless otherwise indicated, scripture is taken from the King James Version.'

Finding Jesus After My Storm/Stephanie Defrance Williams

ISBN-13: 978-1-956775-19-8

LCCN:2022903758

Dedication

I WOULD LIKE TO THANK my Father, Jesus Christ, for loving and believing in me. My husband and best friend Jerry Williams, my sister Shirley, my nieces Carlisha and Stephanie, the rest of my family and friends, including both churches in the USA and Ghana. My mentor prophetess Kimberly Moses, spiritual mothers, Pearl Awe, Apostle Jean Matthews, and Daisy Sours. And everyone who has pushed and encouraged me to go deeper in Jesus.

Stephanie Defrance Williams is a sister, encourager, and has a gift of helps and strong discernment. She is married to Jerry Williams and they have one son. They started the Mirror of Christ Ministry in 2020. They furnish equipment for different ministries, provide school supplies, food, and medicines for families in the US and Ghana. Stephanie has served in multiple areas in ministry, but her greatest love is for those who feel like they can never recover after a personal storm. She is an example of an overcomer to anyone who has gone through rejection, molestation, low self-esteem, the loss of a loved one, and depression. One day she decided not to stay in a state of depression. She got closer to God and told Him whatever it took to be totally healed, she would do it. Her passion is to be effective in ministry to bring about deliverance and wholeness in the body of Christ.

TABLE OF CONTENTS

INTRODUCTION..................................1
CHAPTER 1: My Family........................3
CHAPTER 2: My Mother.......................8
CHAPTER 3: Molestation....................11
CHAPTER 4: Insecurities...................15
CHAPTER 5: Married for Healing..........19
CHAPTER 6: Forgiveness...................23
CHAPTER 7: A Chance to Show Love That I Did Not Experience As A Child..........................26
CHAPTER 8: Developing A Relationship With God and Overcoming Church Hurt.............................29
CHAPTER 9: The Saddest Day of My Life.....35
CHAPTER 10: When It Rains It Pours.............44
CHAPTER 11: Journey To Healing..................47
CHAPTER 12: Learning To Really Walk In Forgiveness..........................52
ABOUT THE AUTHOR..60

Introduction

*W*HILE WRITING THIS BOOK, I endure great warfare! My computer broke twice. My transcripts were erased and some pages were missing. "Finding Jesus After My Storm," was birth as part of my healing journey. Anyone called in ministry and wants to be effective for Jesus needs to be totally healed and have no residual hurts from their past. So for me, that included healing from the death of my niece, church hurt and childhood hurt too. One Sunday morning at my church, they had a guest speaker who was a Prophet. I wasn't interested in what he heard from God because I felt God had failed me due to my niece's passing. After he finished preaching, he started praying for people. He saw me and said, "The lady wearing a white flower can I pray for you?" At first, I acted like I didn't know he was talking to me and started looking around. My friend sitting next to me reassured me he was talking to me. The church I attended was small and I was known for always wearing flowers in my hair. I didn't want to get up, but since I was in church, I said to myself, "You better be obedient." So he began to prophesy about something that happened in my family that shook my faith and that one day I would write about it in a book. I put it on the back burner. After connecting with Prophetess K and Tron Moses' ministry, it was prophesied again. Not only by her but other ministers connected to her ministry as well. I can remember it like yesterday. I was reading one of her books called, "In Right Standing." I couldn't stop crying and repenting through each chapter. I also said to the Lord, "Hey! There's something wrong with me." So I chose to be totally healed by whatever way the Lord would do it. If it meant I would be uncomfortable, I was ready for this journey. My prayer is that someone will be encouraged by my transparency and realize that even through the darkest storm, Jesus is with them and they will survive.

CHAPTER 1

My Family

*E*XODUS 20:12 SAYS (KJV), "Honour thy father and thy mother: that thy days may be long upon the land which the Lord thy God giveth thee."

Both of my parents were from Texarkana, Arkansas. My mom was the baby out of five children. Her mother died when she was a baby of Tuberculosis. My mom had a third grade education, but she desired to become a teacher. Since she had to help her family pick cotton to survive, she could not go back to school. I don't know much about my dad's family except his father was a white Frenchman. My parents moved to Southern California for a better way of life. At that time, they had three children and my mother was pregnant with my sister Shirley. My parents didn't stay there long because my aunt persuaded them to move to a small town located in central California called Corcoran. According to my older sister Jesse, my aunt had promised to help my parents, but she didn't do anything when they arrived.

My mother was an exceptionally beautiful woman. She was tall and dark skinned with freckles on her face, which I thought was cool. I was her seventh child out of nine children. I can remember when my mom used to play with all of us. That was a joyful time in my life. Looking back, she was also a heavy drinker and depressed. She would buy one pint of Vodka and have these yelling and crying spells because she didn't know how she was going to raise her nine children. My father was tall, very handsome, and mixed with French and African American. He was a womanizer who loved all races of women. My older siblings said they witnessed my dad physically and verbally abuse my mom. I remember how my mother used to tell me how my dad would tell her she was too black and ugly which really hurt her. She had to get government assistance because he had left her and wasn't supporting her. For extra money, she worked as a maid or cook. My dad would pop up every now and then only to have sex. I remember my mother begging, crying, and telling my dad how she needed money for food for us. He lied and told her he did not have any money. I must have been seven or eight years old. I was playing with my younger brother Shantay. I ran around my dad and grabbed his pants back pocket and his wallet fell out with a lot of money in it. I remember thinking how I would never beg anyone for money, especially a man.

Since my mom's mother died from Tuberculous during her youth, she grew close to her siblings. However, the brother and sister she was closed to were both murdered. I remember my uncle Dean. He was nice and in the army. I remember when my mom and aunt had to go to Los Angeles to pick up his personal belongings because he was found stabbed to death in a hotel. My Aunt Catherine, who was pretty much like a mother to my mother, was shot by her jealous boyfriend as my mom witnessed it. My mom said she was trying to warn her. She was pregnant at the time with my sister Catherine and went into premature labor. When I was younger, I could not understand why my mom did certain things. Now that I am older, I understand she was just trying to cope with all that hurt in her own way.

My aunt Catherine had three teenage daughters when she passed. My mom could not care for them financially so they went to my aunt. Two of the girls ran away and got married but the youngest one stayed. When she got older, she would get drunk and curse my aunt out at family gatherings. She behaved this way for years and my mom would calm her down. I was told that my aunt forced her into prostitution and mistreated her. This aunt did not like any of us as a matter of fact. She even tried to turn some of us against our mother. She was into witchcraft and our cousins felt like they were better than us and used to make fun of us. Many times, we suffered from no food while she did well. She owned a small farm and her house. One day she did buy us some food, but it was all fat from one of her pigs and my mom had to pay her back for that. I had a great aunt who cheated my mom and aunt out of some land left to them by their

My Family

grandmother. She was treated special because she was half white. I was told that I looked like my grandmother. She was called Red because she was tall and light skinned with freckles on her face.

PRAYER:

Lord, I come against generational curses in my family in the name of Jesus and I forgive all of those who spoke word curses against my family and me. Father, I thank you for the power of forgiveness and I seal this prayer with your blood in Jesus' precious name. Amen.

CHAPTER 2

My Mother

ATTHEW 6:15 (KJV) SAYS, "But if ye forgive not men their trespasses, neither will your Father forgive your trespasses."

My mom loved drinking Vodka with Orange juice and had a bad temper. Daily she would curse people out if she felt they disrespected her. I can recall my mother drinking not just on weekends but every day. She left us alone sometimes for days. She would give us instructions not to answer the phone or door. One night this big guy who would hide in the bushes in our yard sometimes tried to bust down our front door because his family only let him outside at night time. When I was younger, families who had relatives with mental problems would keep them at home in the day and let them out at night. My mom was out on one of her rendezvous with her friend Karen one night. That night when he tried to come in, the window on the door was broken. The curtain was covering the broken window but he tried several times. My siblings and I were in a corner, afraid and shaking. Finally, he gave up and left. Three days later when my mom arrived home, we all tried to explain what happened, but she was very nonchalant about the whole incident. Two months later, that guy was caught having sex with some farm animals and was committed to a mental hospital. My mom had her favorites in the family: my two older brothers, my older sister, and two younger brothers. She would go to their basketball games and give them whatever they wanted. My two older sisters and I would also join the swim team during the summer. Numerous times my mom would make excuses to avoid attending our swim meets. Prior to the age of ten, I remember having a close and loving relationship with my mom but it changed. Before she used to play with me and I would be so happy. Then she started pushing me away and that would hurt me.

PRAYER:

Lord, I forgive my mother for not loving me like her favorites. God Thank You because you have no favorites and you love everyone the same. So Father thank You for allowing me to forgive. I seal this prayer in Jesus' precious name. Amen.

CHAPTER 3

Molestation

MATTHEW 18:21-22 (KJV) SAYS, "Then came Peter to him, and said Lord, How oft shall my brother sin against me, and I forgive him? till seven times? Jesus saith unto him, I say not unto thee, Until seven times: but Until seventy times seven."

My mother and father were separated and my mother started dating Mr. Jackson. He was older, rich, and married. I can recall how my older siblings would ask her to stop dating him because they were being talked about. One of my sisters would get in fights every day because some high school kids would call my mom bad names. The town we grew up in was small and everyone knew each other's business, but my mother kept dating Mr. Jackson. She would tell us to walk with our heads up because people were jealous of her. I remember thinking, "How can my siblings and I be proud when our mother is dating someone else's husband?" He started molesting me when I was eight years old and it lasted until I was 15 years old. The old man would kiss and touch me inappropriately. He told me how he wanted to take me away. My mom was crazy about him and did whatever he asked. When he would come over to see my mom, they would be in her bedroom. She would call me in there to comb his hair. I had to continue this routine each time he came to see my mother. I never told anyone what he was doing because I thought what he was doing to me was my fault. I felt dirty and ashamed, so I buried those feelings by being the class clown in school. I didn't want to think about what was happening to me when I got home.

Mrs. White was a teacher's aide who always invited me to her church. So one day I went and enjoyed it. The third time I attended, I accepted Jesus as my Savior at 15 years old and that following Sunday, I got baptized. I then realized what

Molestation

Mr. Jackson was doing was wrong, so I decided to tell my mom. I was watching one of my favorite singers on American Bandstand and he had just finished singing his song, "What You Won't Do For Love." My mom had finished cooking and I told her I needed to talk to her about what Mr. Jackson had been doing to me. She became very irate and told me I was lying and trying to destroy her relationship. She chased me outside and then tried to throw some hot grease on me. My relationship with my mother had changed when she started dating Mr. Jackson. After that incident, a part of me felt like she didn't exist anymore. Around that time, my mother's health changed. My mom had high blood pressure, but she would never take her medication because she enjoyed drinking. She damaged her kidneys at only 42 years old. When my mother's physical appearance started changing because of the dialysis three times a week, Mr. Jackson did not want her anymore, so he left her.

My mom was not particularly a good mother. Not only did I get molested, but my other siblings suffered abuse too. One of them told me they couldn't remember when it started because she blocked it out. She said she recalled how when we didn't have any food in our house. Mr. Jackson would buy cup of noodles, boloney, and bread and line her up with our other siblings. He told them they could have the food if she would call him daddy. My sister said she never did it. Mr. Jackson did this several times and she never gave in. He even asked my mom to ask my sister if she wanted to start taking birth control pills at 16 years old so she could make some money. My sister told my mom no. When my sister would see Mr. Jackson in the street, her friends and her would curse him out and tell him he was a pervert. Mr. Jackson would then tell my mom. My sister would get a beating and choked out by my mother. My mom would say to her that if he wasn't happy then she wasn't happy. My mother was a woman who was focused on pleasing her man.

PRAYER:

Father, I don't understand why I had to go through all the abuse from my mother and Mr. Jackson. Yet Father, I choose to forgive. I thank You and seal this prayer in Jesus' name. Amen.

CHAPTER 4

Insecurities

John 8:44 (KJV) says, "Ye are of your father the devil, and the lusts of your father ye will do. He was a murderer from the beginning, and abode not in the truth, because there is no truth in him. When he speaketh a lie, he speaketh of his own: for he is a liar, and the father of it.

I moved to Pasadena, California to live with my two older sisters, Jessie and Shirley when I was finishing my last year of high school. I was able to graduate there too. After being molested, I suffered from low self-esteem and never thought I was pretty. One day I was walking back from the store and was stopped by this guy. His name was Avo. He was Armenian and had lied about his age. He told me that I was beautiful. I was 19 years old and so naive. He flattered me with sweet words and validated me. I was only attracted to Middle Eastern and Caucasian European men because when I was young black guys always told me I was ugly, fat, not light enough, and my hair was not good enough.

When I came to Southern California, European and Middle Eastern men would try to date me, but some were looking for a green card. After a month, Avo made a lot of promises that never came true. He was my first love. He would only see me on weekdays after 5 pm because he said he was busy fixing cars. One day when he came inside my apartment to meet my older sister Jessie he was so nervous. He would not look her in the face. So, when I came back later from the motel, my sister told me he was married. I became angry with her and told her he was not. She left me alone and did not say anything else. Looking back, she knew I was naive and in love.

I was a Christian only in name. I was faithful in paying my tithes and offering but not in a relationship with the Lord because I wasn't ready to give Jesus my whole heart. Avo just wanted

Insecurities

me for sex which made me feel bad. He would buy me fast food and take me to a cheap motel out of town. When I would try to call his number on the weekends, he would never pick up. Later I realized that was the number to his job. I started feeling that maybe he was married because he started acting strange. So something told me to tell him I missed my period and I also may be pregnant.

Looking back now, I believe it was the Holy Spirit. When I told him that, he became nervous and said that I didn't need a baby and abort it. So then I asked him if he was married and he said yes and he had two kids. My heart sank! He also told me he did not want to see me anymore! I remember crying. He drove me home. I began telling him how I didn't care that he was married because I loved him but deep down, I knew I couldn't ever be comfortable with him. I remember how as a kid, my mom dated Mr. Jackson who was married. My siblings and I were so embarrassed in our small town, so I made it a rule that I wouldn't date married men because I wouldn't want anyone dating my husband.

FINDING JESUS AFTER MY STORM

Some guys would lie to me but when I found out they were married I would not see them again. For months I cried over Avo. I would date but they were rebounds. One year later, Avo called me. I saw him just two more times and then I left him alone because he would never be mine. I decided to get serious about life and improve my status from working as a nurse's aide to a Licensed Vocational Nurse (LVN). So, I enrolled in a private school located in Los Angeles. During that time, I wanted to get married and have children.

PRAYER:

Lord, I Thank You because You said in Psalms 139:14 that I am fearfully and wonderfully made. Father, I Thank You because You love me for me and I am special to you always. You never make mistakes and I seal this prayer with Jesus' Blood. Amen!

CHAPTER 5

Married For Healing

PSALMS 34:18 (NIV) SAYS, "The Lord is close to the brokenhearted and saves those who are crushed in spirit."

While attending school for my LVN, one of my classmates and I became study partners. She asked what kind of men I liked. I was 22 years old and some of my friends were getting married, having kids, and looked so happy. I wanted that too. My classmate introduced me to this Indian guy named Ishmael Mohammed. He was cute and studying to be an Engineer. We started dating and in less than two months, we got married at the courthouse. I thought by marrying him, I would have a good life and forget my childhood pain. He was my prince just like in the fairy tale stories. After we got married, I moved into his apartment. I asked him where our marriage license was the second night because I wanted to hang it up. He became startled and said it was at his older brother's house. I asked, "Why?" He started stumbling over his words, so it was clear to me he was lying. Finally, I asked him why he really married me. He alleged only for his green card. He responded by saying, yes 50% he loved me and 50% for his green card. We got into a bad argument and he slapped me. He then told me that no one was going to marry me because I was not a virgin. He insisted that he was doing me a favor by marrying him.

Well, I started to cry, jumped on the bus and went back home to Pasadena. I was living with Shirley before I got married and I told her I would divorce him. I finished up LVN school and took the state exam, then passed. However, Ishmael continued to try to bribe me to help him get his green card and I kept telling him no. Even after our divorce, he kept trying to get back with me. I had to threaten him and that is how he left me alone. Our classmate was a liar because I found out later that she knew he needed his green card. She was really a recruiter who got paid for finding Americans to marry foreigners for citizenship. After that, I had a hate for Indians and foreigners. If any of them asked me out, I would ask if they had their green card. I was very bitter. Some of the guys were legit. They were either lawyers or doctors. They would tell me they did not need a green card, but I was still angry and thought I should start dating black guys. I must have been desperate because most of them did not have a job and I was helping them financially. I had to deal with some baby mama drama too.

This one guy I dated, our relationship became very serious. I thought we would get married even though he was a womanizer and lied about giving me a STD. Thank God it was cured by medication. We made a date to look at the wedding rings on Saturday. He never showed up or answered my calls. He would disappear for 1 to 2 months sometimes. He would tell me he was visiting his aunt or helping her. I found out he was with his other woman or sometimes in jail on the weekends for unpaid tickets. Also, I could not trust him because he would try to talk to my friends and talk about my weight which made me feel bad. Finally, I decided I would stop allowing these guys to disrespect and lie to me. So, I started eating differently, walking and hiking. I lost over 100 pounds and decided to get serious about my relationship with God. At times I would fornicate but when I got in my late 30s I said it was enough. I began to put my focus on the Lord.

PRAYER:

Lord, I decree Psalms 51:10 that says create in me a clean heart and renew a right spirit. Father, I ask that you remove any bitterness from my heart from anyone who has lied or used me. I know I have to forgive because I want to be pleasing in Your sight so Thank You for not allowing me to hold on to any bitterness or unforgiveness in my heart. I seal this prayer with your blood in Jesus' name. Amen.

CHAPTER 6

Forgiveness

MATTHEW 25:35-36 (NIV) SAYS, "For I was hungry and you gave me something to eat, I was thirsty and you gave me something to drink, I was a stranger and you invited me in, I needed clothes and you clothed me, I was sick and you looked after me, I was in prison and you came to visit me."

My mother needed someone to help care for her because being on dialysis three times a week made her weak. She was confined to a wheelchair and needed financial help. Some of our siblings caring for her were taking advantage of her. Even though I came from a big family, some of my siblings were doing better financially. Shirley and I agreed to care for her while everyone else wanted to put her in a convalescent home. So Shirley and my niece Christina, who was five years old, went down to Corcoran, our home town to care for her. I would come later, and sent money to help pay the bills.

It was not easy for us to care for our mother because we were not her favorite. We were both Christians now and had to do what God said, which was to honor your father and mother. Shirley had to remove some of our siblings because they were very disrespectful to our mother. The week I was going to move to Corcoran. I got a call from Shirley. She said when she went into our mother's room to help get her ready for dialysis, she was not responding. She realized my mom had passed away in her sleep. Shirley told me that she was able to talk about some of the things that happened to her when she was a child. My mother cried and told her she was sorry. Shirley led her to the Lord. The night before she died, Shirley said she woke up from her sleep because she heard my mother talking to someone and looking up at the corner of the ceiling. She told her to go back to bed because the chariots were there to pick her up and she

Forgiveness

would be fine. Well, the next day, mom passed away in her sleep.

PRAYER:

Lord, I Thank you for allowing Shirley and I to help our mother and also to forgive her. Father, we thank you for restoring our relationship with our mom before she passed away and for showing her love. Father, I Thank you and seal all these prayers with your blood. Amen.

CHAPTER 7

A Chance To Show Love That I Did Not Experience As a Child

Psalm 127:3 (NIV) says, "Children are a heritage from the Lord, offspring a reward from him."

I would have to say one of the happiest days of my life was helping to raise my three nieces. I know there is a saying that says hurt people hurt people. But for me, that was not true. Even though I suffered abuse as a child, my lifelong dream was to have children or to show love to abused children. One day, my sister and I received a call from a social worker in San Bernardino, California. She told us that my sister Catherine held these two young babies while walking into traffic. She went on to say that they had to put them in foster care, and if my sister and I did not want to get them, two different families wanted to adopt them. We said no adoption and we took and raised them. Shirley already had Christina. She was an only child for a long time. So, having two little people come into her space was not easy at first, but it worked out fine because we treated them equally. I told Shirley because of the babysitting issues the state would take a while to help them.

I was already working as an LVN. She just needed to concentrate on being a mother to all the kids. So, we raised the kids together. We took them to school, signed them up for the boys and girls club, basketball, swimming, and music. We took them hiking, horseback riding, to the beach, to church and the movies and we used to sneak snacks inside too. I really love celebrating their birthdays because I used to love to dance with them and we made sure we attended all their games and school activities. We also participated in parent teacher conferences. When they misbehaved in class, we would take turns sitting in their class. We would always remind them that they could become anything they wanted to be in life. We told them to always keep God first and get a good education no matter their background.

PRAYER:

Father, I Thank You for allowing me to help raise my nieces and not allowing them to ever go through the trauma I had endured as a child. Father, I thank you for giving me one of my greatest joys. I seal this prayer with your blood. Amen.

CHAPTER 8

Developing A Relationship With God and Overcoming Church Hurt

MATTHEW 11:28 (KJV) COME unto me, all ye that labour and are heavy laden, and I will give you rest.

I started attending the Church Of God on and off when I was 19. When I was working as a CNA, my coworker invited me. The Pastor and his wife were so nice. They were not stuck up like other Pastors I had encountered. I was fine just paying my tithes and offerings. I felt people who came to church had to be perfect. Also, different Christians had told me I wasn't good enough because my parents were not together, God honors Christians that have a mother and father and were given a special anointing for it. It wasn't until my mid-twenties that I started staying and listening to the whole service because I would leave before the benediction. When the Pastor's wife brought to my attention what I was doing because she had noticed it, I stopped. I felt she was a very nice lady who cared about me.

One day the Pastor asked if he could talk to me. Well, that meeting turned into a couple of years of counseling sessions. He showed me in God's Word how the Lord loved me, and the molestation was not my fault. I started really getting involved in church. Shirley was looking for a new church, so she and my nieces started coming to church with me. Some of the ushers and members were so mean. Some women thought that because my sister and I were single, we were after their husbands. One of the members asked me out to lunch, but when I asked, "Your wife will be there too right?" He hung up the phone.

Shirley and I became active in church: cleaning, serving, and putting on dinners for the seniors. We really grew to love our pastor and his family. His wife became my good friend, but they moved away because he was offered a higher position in the Church Of God organization. I was heartbroken and I did become too dependent on him. But before he left, he asked Shirley and I to be at church that following Sunday morning because we needed to vote in the new pastor. Only the tithe payers were allowed to vote. We were so surprised because only seven of us were there and we had over 200 members in the church. Some of them were very well off and had good jobs.

When the new young pastors arrived from back East, they were cool at first, so we were very supportive. One day at a church meeting, he talked about how he thought it was a good idea to buy a hotel. He even brought in his old pastor to talk to us about it because his church owned one. Well, we never heard about the hotel anymore. A couple of years later, they purchased a beautiful mansion. The tithe payers never knew about the mansion until after they bought it. It was alleged that the pastor's wife inherited money from her dad. I was upset and so were some of the members. I remember when the pastor said he didn't need a board but just trust him. Looking back, I wouldn't be under a leader like that again. He did have his five special friends on his pastoral team. There was a change in the Pastor and his wife after they bought the mansion. The church was getting bigger and multicultural, which was cool. The pastor and his wife were disrespectful to some of the seniors and some of the members. As a result, some people left. It was bad. They changed from being a God pleaser to people pleasers.

One Sunday morning while I was worshiping, I felt this heaviness and then I heard a voice telling me I wouldn't be back. After church, I kept crying and heard it again I wouldn't be back. I told God I couldn't go because I had been there since I was 19 years old and now I was in my 30s. I knew if I continued being there, things would be worse for me. My sister and I noticed the pastor and his wife were compromising. I wrote my resignation and gave it to the assistant pastor. I left the church hurt and saw a lot of favoritism too.

So Shirley, the kids and I visited churches and fell in love with this multicultural Four Square Church. This church operated in the prophetic, hearing God's voice, and speaking in tongues. They taught that those gifts were for everyone. It wasn't long that this Prophetess befriended me and I became her armor bearer. I learned a lot from her, but I thought she was more special to God because she was a prophet. I was able to go around the prophetic circle. I saw some of them milking people for money and justifying their wrongdoing. The Prophetess I assisted had a lot of pride and she didn't believe in paying tithes and offering. I witnessed her arguing with some people, telling them she was a prophet. Finally, I had to let her go because I was getting dependent on her and she felt that there were no good pastors left, which was scary.

The pastor and his wife were so cool. I remember when his mom and him went to one of my niece's Christian basketball games. She was so happy. We stayed at the church for 5 years and God said it was time to move on and we didn't leave there angry. I learned about Jesus in a deeper way at this church. My two oldest nieces were away at college and Carlisha was in town. I started attending this small multicultural church with Shirley and even started ushering. The people were nice at first, but they didn't move in the Gifts of the Spirit. They enjoyed drinking and gossiping, but we stayed because we knew there was no perfect church.

PRAYER:

Lord, I Thank You for allowing me to learn from each church you have led me to because it allowed me to grow and trust You. Father, I Thank You for allowing me to realize there is no perfect church. Thank You Father and I seal this prayer with your Blood. Amen.

CHAPTER 9

The Saddest Day of My Life

ISAIAH 43:2 (KJV) SAYS, "When thou passest through the waters, I will be with thee; and through the rivers, they shall not overflow thee: when thou walkest through the fire, thou shalt not be burned; neither shall the flame kindle upon thee."

After the death of my mom, my siblings went their own ways. Shirley and I heard from some of them when they needed financial help. One day my oldest sister's best friend told me that she had been sick and in the hospital for one year. She almost died. She lived in Los Angeles, which was fifteen miles away, but we hadn't talked in years because of my mother and other things.

I always wanted to see my sister, so I asked for her number, called her and made plans to see her. Shirley, my nieces, and I went to see her. I started crying because I was so happy to see her and her children. It was great for my nieces to bond with their first cousins. They look so much alike. My sister had lost a lot of weight. She had kidney failure and other medical problems. She didn't take her medication for her high blood pressure because her children's father had a problem with her gaining weight. She would take diet pills, which was not good. She also had to be on dialysis three times a week. After seeing her, I made sure I didn't miss out on any more time with her.

My oldest brother was close to a few of my siblings. He was big on education. If a person didn't have a Masters like him or a Bachelors, he felt they were nothing. I found out he passed of colon cancer from his pastor's wife. His wife never told us he was sick. When Jessie spoke to her on the phone, she said he didn't want us to know. The pastor's wife told me he had repented before he passed. He had a very big funeral. My

The Saddest Day of My Life

siblings and I would have loved to attend, but I'm glad he was saved.

Jessie decided she wanted to go to our home town for a visit. She hadn't been there since she was eighteen years old. One Saturday, we drove down there with her son, grandkids, and my niece Carlisha. We plan to drop my sister Catherine off at her home because she lived down there, but first, we visited our aunt. When she saw us she asked if we brought any money! She had not changed but was still money hungry. After we visited our aunt, we took Catherine home. She was down visiting and wanted to make some tacos for us. When we arrived at her house, there was no food. She tried to say her roommate ate all the food. Catherine had been doing drugs since she was fourteen years old. I could tell the area she lived in was full of drug users. So Jessie gave her money to buy food. She was a great cook. I often wonder why she did drugs. I was told by one of my sisters that Mr. Jackson had molested her too. When we finished eating, we drove back home. I noticed that Jessie wanted to take pictures. She said it was for memories, but I felt she wouldn't live long.

After two weeks, she was admitted back and forth to the hospital. Before she could be released home, she had to go to a convalescent hospital in Highland Park, ten minutes away from Pasadena. Shirley and I would go there and care for her. She got discharged and came home, but she was back in the hospital a week later. Hearing God's voice became stronger to me. I was still doubting myself. The Lord told me that my sister wasn't going to last long and make sure she is secure in her salvation. I blew it off but my friend who was a Prophet and Pastor in Ghana called me at 1 a.m. He confirmed what the Lord told me. The next morning I went to the hospital. She started telling me how she was upset with the landlord because she had lied and done some shady things to her. I talked to her about the importance of forgiveness and repentance. She repented and forgave her landlord. I could see my sister was getting weaker and I asked her if she was okay. She told me she was and that she spoke to Jesus every night. When she asked me the same questions, I held back tears, lied and said yes. She had me to promise that I would check on my nephew when she passed. He was very attentive to my sister and a mom's boy.

The Saddest Day of My Life

My sister had signed paper work in the hospital that when her condition changed, she did not want to be on any life-support. When I left the hospital, the Lord told me her condition would change that Friday. It did and two weeks later, I had to decide with her children to take her off of the ventilator. It was a few days after her fifty fifth birthday.

Christian and Stephanie were star athletes in grade school and college. Carlisha was good at sports too, but she liked music and going to movies more. Christian and Stephanie were out of state going to college after they had completed two years of junior college. Carlisha was in college too. Christian had this coach she loved like a father. He reassured her that she had a basketball scholarship to attend there. After a week, she would call home. Her mom and I could tell how unhappy she was. She never had any money and we would send her some. I called the school and spoke to a gentleman in the financial department regarding my niece's scholarship. The gentleman endorsed to me that my niece didn't have a scholarship. Her financial aid was paying for her college. I told my sister and my niece what

I had found out. My niece came back home. She said she wasn't playing basketball anyway and she hated that college. I wasn't happy about her decision and I talked to Shirley about it. She told me to stay out of it.

As my nieces got older, I could see that they thought I was mean and overprotective. I was so determined to not allow my niece to suffer like I had as a child. So I promised myself I would pour into them and make sure they all graduated from the University. My niece started working when she got back home at the Pasadena Center. At this center, they believe in giving felons a second chance. My nieces knew how to work and liked having their own money. They all have good social skills. My niece met Tabatha at her job. My nieces always brought their friends to the house and some even stayed with us when they fell on hard times. We didn't charge them rent as long as they just continued going to college, but a few were users and my sister had them to leave.

The first time my niece brought Tabatha to meet us, I felt a very evil presence. I tried to

The Saddest Day of My Life

shake it off, but each time she came over I felt the same way. I didn't know anything about her background. I had a strong feeling if my niece continued hanging out with her, she would go to prison or wind up dead. It wasn't until later my sister told me she had been involved in a murder with some other kids when she was fourteen years old. My niece got arrested for driving a stolen car and had to spend one month in a correctional detention center in Lakewood, California. I recall when she was sentenced, the Public Defender said she had two witnesses that saw my niece steal the car. After the judge heard the car was Tabatha's and everyone in the car had a record, including the witnesses, he said that they set my niece up. So he sentenced my niece to teach her a lesson.

When Carlisha and I visited my niece in the correctional center, I held back tears because she had never gotten in any trouble like that. She was so naive, trusting, book smart, but not street smart. Tabatha was sent back to prison for one year because she violated parole. After my niece had gotten out of jail, Tabatha's family would leave phone messages asking her to leave money on the books for her. I stayed out of it because I could not make my niece do anything. After Tabatha got out of jail, my niece felt Tabatha went to jail for her. I tried to convince her that wasn't true. So she helped her pay for a hotel because she couldn't get along with her family. My sister told me the night before my niece was murdered that this homeless man walked up to my niece. He asked her if she knew who Jesus was and told her that she had a personal angel.

I can recall that day when I answered the house phone. The person on the phone tried to disguise their voice, but when they asked if my niece was home I felt something bad had happened to my niece. Before I left for work and when I arrived, I kept trying to call my niece, but it kept going to voicemail. When I got to work, I was very restless. I even asked my niece Carlisha and sister to try to call Christian. When I got home the next morning, she told me to sit down and two detectives had come to the house early in the morning. Christian was in the County Morgue and the murder was all caught on tape. It showed Tabatha stabbing my niece several times, kicking, and dragging her body in the motel room. She let her bleed to death, then called 911 and told them someone had been hurt at the motel, but she didn't know which room. Once my sister told me that my niece was in the morgue, I felt Tabatha killed her just like she was involved in the killing when she was fourteen years old. She was found the next day and arrested. My sister didn't want a big long funeral. We had a memorial service fast. We were disappointed in some of our church family and close friends that didn't support us in our time of need, but I thank the Lord for the ones and my coworkers He allowed to help us.

PRAYER:

Lord, I love You, and You know how much I miss Christian's smile and her laugh. I miss her saying Aunt Steph or Aunt Stephanie look at this or that, but you remind me I have to live and finish my God given assignment and I will see her again. Thank You for healing my heart. Lord, I Bless Tabatha and her family. I pray they will all be saved before they leave this earth. So Father I Thank You and seal this prayer with the blood of Jesus. Amen!

CHAPTER 10

When it Rains It Pours

*I*SAIAH 26:3 (KJV) SAYS, "Thou wilt keep him in perfect peace, whose mind is stayed on thee: because he trusteth in thee."

One month after my niece's death, the orphanage in Ghana that I was a part of with Jerry and other friends was closed. Seventeen children had to go to a government orphanage. The pastor we were helping there stole the money that was to be used for a school, clinic, and a new orphanage. He used the money to buy a new house and church in Ghana. He also remarried. Looking back, my friends and I were just too trusting. We didn't pray before connecting with this pastor.

After my niece's death, I took a month off from work to spend time with my sister. When I returned to work, I was functioning but depressed. Some of my coworkers signed a petition to remove the LVN position. I was hurt because some of those RNs used to be a LVN that I helped train. Some LVNs were removed, but I was able to stay because I found favor with my boss. I was also a victim of identity theft. I had to spend so much time fixing that problem. It was a mess! My friend Jerry who I didn't like at first because he was African, helped me. I worked with many Africans and heard so many stories about how they use American women. I swore that I would never marry one, but Jerry would always call to check on me during my difficult times. I have known him since 2010, but we became good friends at the end of 2011 and in 2016, we got married in Ghana.

PRAYER:

Lord, I forgive the Pastor, co-workers, and the person who stole my identity. Lord, I don't understand why some people do bad things, but I Thank You for allowing me to forgive people who have hurt me. Father, I Thank You for allowing me to marry Jerry because he loves me for me. Lord, I Thank you and I seal this prayer with your blood. Amen.

CHAPTER 11

Journey to Healing

*P*SALM 147:3 (KJV) SAYS, "He healeth the broken in heart, and bindeth up their wounds."

After two years, my sister Shirley started watching a lot of preaching on YouTube. She kept telling me about this young, blonde, bubbly, Afro-American Prophetess. Her name was Prophetess Kimberly Hargraves. My sister told me she used to be an Exotic Dancer, was studying to become a doctor, but God called her into full time ministry. My sister asked me to help her subscribe to her email and YouTube channel. Shirley would tell me that this prophetess reminded her of me. So I looked her up and I thought she was a pretty nineteen or twenty year old. I thought, "What could I learn from this kid." I didn't like her. It wasn't that she was an ex-exotic dancer. Let me shame the devil and tell the truth! At one time, I really wanted to be an exotic dancer and my stage name was going to be Delicious! I didn't pursue it because I was too afraid. I had worked with a prophetess for five years and traveled around the city with her in the Prophetic Circle. I saw some of them manipulate and lie to people for money. That left a bitter taste in my mouth towards Prophets. I was still hurting about my niece's death and going to church yet dealing with hurt. I was mad at the church and God. I wasn't interested in being a part of any ministry.

My sister tried to get me to see Prophetess Kimberly and I would blow her off. I noticed my sister liked this Prophetess and she doesn't usually take to everyone. One day I decided to watch her. She was teaching on the prophets of the Bible and prophesying. I was impressed so Shirley and I started buying her books. One day I told my sister I saw her prophesying at her job in the closet on her lunch break! She told me she was probably avoiding getting in any trouble. My sister was very adamant about investing in this Prophetess' ministry. When she had her conference, Shirley asked my husband and I if we could help donate things for the conference. So I contacted her and we donated some things. I really didn't mind because It was therapeutic for me.

I had just lost another family member. One day I was reading Prophetess Kimberly's book, In Right Standing. I cried and repented all through that book. I recall telling Jesus, "Hey! There is something wrong with me!" I realized I needed healing from some deep hurts. So I told the Lord I wanted to be healed. Whatever it took or how uncomfortable it felt I would do it. He had me to join Prophetess Kimberly's prayer line. First, I joined the call at noon and later joined the prayer line at six a.m. These calls are on Eastern Standard Time. I live in Southern California so my time zone is Pacific Standard Time. There is a three hour difference. I would complain to the Lord that the people on the prayer line prayed too long, the calls were not clear and they would drop. However, the Lord would tell me don't hang up and call back and I would. He had me join her book club so I could interact with other people. I was going to work, church, hiking, and then back home. I enjoyed reading her books. I have always liked hearing other people's perspective on a subject, but I was a little apprehensive because I didn't know these people and could I be myself? Or were they some Bougie church people? But they were good. God also had me to take her classes: The School of the Prophets and her mentorship class. Those classes helped me to share some deep hurts, be transparent with God, and start a YouTube Channel dealing with healing and walking in Forgiveness. I have learned that if a person really wants to be healed, they have to admit they need help and stop walking in a victim mentality.

PRAYER:

Father, I Thank You for allowing Shirley, Jerry and I to connect to Prophetess K and Pastor Tron's ministry. Father, I pray for what she has done for my family and others, You will do for her whole family. Lord continue to strengthen her family and keep them well. Father, I seal this prayer with your blood in Jesus' name. Amen.

CHAPTER 12

Learning To Really Walk In Forgiveness

ATTHEW 6:15 (KJV) SAYS, "But if ye forgive not men their trespasses, neither will your Father forgive your trespasses."

I had these three rules concerning if I felt anyone disrespected me. Number one: the first time I would let it pass because maybe I did something or maybe the person is having a bad day. The second time I would address the issue before we get to number three. Number three: if it happens a third time, I would exit the friendship, and if the person tried to explain their side

Learning To Really Walk In Forgiveness

of the story, I would tell them the conversation was over, walk away, or hang up the phone. I would never speak to the person again and could sit next to the person. I would only speak to them if I had to. But being a Christian, I couldn't do that anymore. I had to do it God's way.

My sister, husband, and I love our friend, who is a Christian Producer with her husband. One day she was interviewing this actress for her movie. I was watching the interview with my sister and another friend. After the interview was over, I texted my friend about how she looked uninterested while interviewing the other lady. Well, she texted me back and it was nasty. She accused me of gossiping and being messy. I was hurt when I received that text and I cried for six days. I felt like she threw a dagger in my heart. I apologized to her and she accepted it. She had really rubbed me the wrong way. That was the second time she had accused me of being something that wasn't true.

Secondly, my sister, husband, and I supported her and her husband's production company for a while. Thirdly, when I would hear any negative things about her or her husband, I would ask my family to pray for them or see how we could help them. Fourthly, I love hard. I told my husband about what happened and he was sad, but I didn't tell my sister. After we gave our friends the equipment we promised them for their company, I had planned to exit the friendship and never speak to her again. I didn't care what we had sown into their ministry or what they had done for us. I was going to go! When I told my prayer partner what had happened, they listened and explained why the friend got upset because she felt I was attacking her.

Also, the Lord told me how some people had left her production company and talked bad about her and her husband. Thank God for true friends because they will tell you the truth in love. Good or bad. I really wanted to hold onto the offense, but when Jesus had shown me I was at fault, I couldn't. I'm not ashamed to say I'm sorry or admit my mistake. I made a promise to Jesus that I would always walk in forgiveness. So I sat on my bed with tears running down my face. I told Jesus if being misunderstood, being called names, and offended caused me to walk

Learning To Really Walk In Forgiveness

in a deeper level of forgiveness, it was worth it. My focus is to please Him and walk in total forgiveness.

One of the things that the Lord had me do was continue to pray with my prayer partner against the spirit of offense, sow seeds and name them. One day during prayer, the Lord spoke through my prayer partner to buy my friend a gift, which was great because her birthday was in a few days. The Lord told me what to get her. She thanked me and said I didn't have to give her the gifts and we were cool. I told her I did what Jesus told me to do. We still love and support our friend and her husband.

Sometimes when a person is not secure in who God has called them, they will use people to get what they want. Unfortunately it happens in ministry too. One day this new member came to our church and she stood up during testimony service and said God had given her a dream about my pastor and she needed to connect with her. We became friends and she even told me that God showed her that we would have a friendship. She was excited about the church and really wanted to know how she could help. I was excited too because I knew the pastor needed some things for her ministry. When she became ill and had to be in admitted into the hospital, I would call her every day and check on her until she was discharged. One thing that made me uncomfortable about her was she kept asking me personal questions about the pastor, which I didn't like because I felt she should ask for herself. She attended a conference with my pastor. My sister and I were happy to donate because she would be setting up a table and selling some things.

When she returned, I called her. I noticed she really didn't want to talk to me. So the next day, I called her and asked her did I do anything wrong. I left her a message. She called me back and reassured me I hadn't done anything wrong and that she was on a 20 day fast. I understood. Well when she got off of the fast, she called me and when I tried to return the call, it went to her voicemail. She texted me one more time after that and when I tried to text her, I saw she blocked me on instant messenger. I left her a phone message apologizing if I did anything wrong forgive me and I would leave her alone.

One of the pastoral staff called me to tell me that the new member had been added to the prayer staff and I responded by saying Amen. I was hurt that the pastor didn't ask me, but I didn't stay hurt long. For fifty six years, I have been overlooked at work and in ministry. I never want to be in a place where I am not welcome. So I have learned just to focus on what God has called me to do. That following Wednesday night, before I got ready to go to church, the Holy Spirit told me she would be praying that night. At my church, we pray Monday through Friday 7 p.m. to 8 p.m. But lately, God has me arriving thirty minutes early to pray by myself to help set the atmosphere. I wasn't going to go, but the Lord told me to face my giant. When she asked anyone if they needed any prayer, I allowed her to pray for my family and I that night. I sensed she was a little uncomfortable. It was pretty evident she used me to get next to the pastor and to have a position.

Finding Jesus after my Storm

One day when I was in prayer, the Holy Spirit allowed me to feel that she was talking about me with other church members. I have no ill feelings towards her. I continue to pray that she gets totally healed and God will continue to use her. My friends know I love to joke around. At my hospital, I was known as the funny lady. It had been over three years since I have been joking with Chelsea regarding her voice because she can really sing beautifully and my sister and I have always loved her name. One day I sent her a text encouraging her. At the end of the text, I said, "I am yet praying for your voice and name," which I usually do. Well she responded back on the voice text asking me was I joking or serious. The rest of the message implied that I wasn't comfortable with myself. I reassured her I was and it had taken me many years to learn to love me. I have to admit I was surprised by this Woman of God. I love her and continue to pray for her.

My nieces say Shirley and I are some of the most forgiving people they know. During the sentence of Tabatha, the lady who murdered my niece, Shirley was closed in the judge's chamber.

Learning To Really Walk In Forgiveness

The judge asked my sister if she had anything to say to Tabatha and my sister said no. The judge was surprised. She even told the District Attorney she forgave Tabatha. Shirley and I pray for her family daily to be saved. For years I always try to teach my nieces to forgive. My sister and I have to walk in it now and it has not been easy. But because our desire is to please God, we will continue to do it.

PRAYER:

Father, Thank You for holding my family through those difficult times and when I felt I couldn't feel you, Father you were there. Father, thank You for allowing me to Forgive no matter how painful the hurt is. Because if I don't forgive the people, you won't forgive me. Father, I love you and I Thank you for this prayer and I seal it with Jesus' blood. Amen.

About The Author

STEPHANIE DE FRANCE WILLIAMS is married to Jerry Williams and they have one son. She has been an LVN for over 30 years and she moves in the gifts of helps, encouragement, strong discernment and the prophetic. With the help of her husband they started the Mirror of Christ Ministry where they help churches and families in college with supplies and equipment. The reason they named their ministry, the Mirror of Christ Ministry, is because they wanted people to see themselves as Christ sees them. God sees us as royalty regardless of our background.

Index

9

911, 44

A

afraid, 9, 49
African, 4, 46
African American, 4
American Bandstand, 13
apartment, 17, 21
Arkansas, 3
Armenian, 16
armor bearer, 34
arrested, 42, 44
ashamed, 12, 55
assistant pastor, 33
aunt, 4, 5, 6, 22, 38
Avo, 16, 17, 18, 19

B

baby, 3, 18, 22
Bachelors, 37
baptized, 12
basketball, 9, 28, 34, 40, 41
basketball games, 9, 34
beautiful, 4, 17, 32
bedroom, 12
benediction, 31
Bible, 49
birth control pills, 14
birthday, 40, 56
birthdays, 29
bitterness, 23
book, 1, 2, 42, 50, 51
broken-hearted, 20
brothers, 9
bushes, 8
business, 11

C

California, 4, 16, 28, 42
Catherine, 5, 6, 28, 38
Caucasian European men, 17
cheated, 6

Index

Chelsea, 59
childhood, 1, 21
children, 3, 4, 19, 28, 37, 40, 45
Christian, 17, 34, 40, 43, 44, 54
Christians, 25, 31
Christina, 25, 28
church, 1, 2, 12, 28, 31, 32, 33, 34, 35, 44, 45, 49, 51, 56, 58, 59
class clown, 12
classmates, 20
colon cancer, 37
computer, 1
conference, 50, 57
Corcoran, 4, 25
correctional detention center, 42
cotton, 3
counseling sessions, 31
cousins, 6, 37
coworker, 30
crying, 2, 4, 5, 18, 33, 37
curtain, 9

D

daddy, 14
dark skinned, 4

death, 1, 5, 36, 44, 45, 46, 49

depressed, 4, 46

dialysis, 13, 24, 25, 37

died, 3, 5, 25, 36

discharged, 39, 57

disrespect, 23

disrespected, 8, 53

District Attorney, 60

doctors, 22

donate, 50, 57

drink, 24

drinker, 4

drugs, 38

E

education, 3, 29, 37

embarrassed, 18

encouraged, 2

ex-exotic dancer, 49

F

family, 2, 3, 6, 7, 8, 9, 24, 32, 42, 43, 44, 50, 51, 55, 58, 60

farm, 6, 9

fast food, 18

father, 3, 4, 11, 16, 25, 31, 37, 40

Index

favorites, 10
financial help, 24, 36
fire, 36
flower, 1
foreigners, 22
forgive, 7, 8, 10, 11, 15, 23, 26, 47, 53, 58, 60
fornicate, 23
foster care, 28
freckles, 4, 7
Frenchman, 3
friend, 1, 9, 20, 32, 36, 39, 46, 54, 55, 56
funeral, 37, 44

G

generational curses, 7
gentleman, 40
Ghana, 39, 45, 46
Gifts of the Spirit, 35
God, 1, 3, 10, 22, 23, 25, 29, 30, 31, 32, 33, 34, 39, 44, 48, 49, 51, 54, 55, 56, 58, 59, 60, 61
gossiping, 35, 54
government assistance, 4
graduation ceremony, 16
grandkids, 38
grandmother, 6, 7

green card, 17, 21, 22
guest speaker, 1

H

hair, 2, 12, 17
happy, 9, 14, 20, 34, 37, 41, 57
healing, 1, 44, 50, 51
health, 13
heart, 18, 23, 44, 48, 54
heartbroken, 32
heritage, 27
high blood pressure, 13, 37
hiking, 23, 28, 51
homeless man, 43
hospital, 36, 39, 40, 57, 59
hot grease, 13
hotel, 5, 32, 43
house, 6, 14, 21, 38, 41, 43, 45
hurt, 1, 4, 6, 9, 27, 33, 44, 46, 47, 49, 54, 58, 60
husband, 12, 19, 50, 54, 55, 56, 61

I

In Right Standing, 2, 50
Indians, 22

instant messenger, 57
Ishmael Mohammed, 20

J

jail, 22, 42, 43
jealous, 5, 12
Jerry, 45, 46, 47, 51, 61
Jesse, 4
Jessie, 16, 17, 37, 38
Jesus, 1, 2, 7, 10, 11, 12, 15, 18, 19, 23, 34, 39, 43, 44, 50, 52, 55, 56, 60
joyful, 4
judge, 42, 59, 60

K

kidneys, 13
kids, 11, 18, 20, 28, 34, 42

L

Lakewood, 42
land, 3, 6
lawyers, 22
liar, 16, 22

Licensed Vocational Nurse, 19
life-support, 40
light skinned, 7
Lord, 2, 3, 7, 10, 11, 17, 19, 20, 23, 25, 26, 27, 31, 35, 39, 40, 44, 47, 50, 51, 55, 56, 58
Los Angeles, 5, 19, 36
love, 10, 17, 19, 26, 28, 29, 32, 34, 44, 54, 55, 56, 59, 60
low self-esteem, 16

M

marriage license, 21
married, 6, 11, 17, 18, 19, 20, 21, 22, 46, 61
Masters, 37
medication, 13, 22, 37
members, 31, 32, 33, 59
mental hospital, 9
mental problems, 8
Middle Eastern men, 17
mind, 45, 50
ministers, 2
ministry, 1, 2, 48, 49, 50, 51, 55, 56, 57, 58, 61
mirror of Christ, 61
mistakes, 19
molested, 13, 16, 38

Index

mom, 3, 4, 5, 6, 8, 9, 11, 12, 13, 14, 18, 25, 26, 34, 36, 39, 40
money, 5, 14, 25, 33, 34, 38, 40, 41, 42, 45, 49
morgue, 43, 44
motel, 17, 18, 43, 44
mother, 3, 4, 5, 6, 8, 10, 11, 12, 13, 14, 24, 25, 26, 28, 31, 37
movies, 28, 40
Mr. Jackson, 11, 12, 13, 14, 18, 38
Mrs. White, 12
murder, 42, 43
murderer, 16
music, 28, 40

N

nervous, 17, 18
niece, 1, 25, 34, 38, 40, 41, 42, 43, 44, 45, 46, 49, 59
nonchalant, 9
noodles, 14

O

obedient, 2
offerings, 31

P

painful, 60
parents, 3, 4, 31
Pasadena, 16, 21, 39, 41
Pastors, 31
people, 1, 8, 12, 27, 28, 31, 33, 34, 35, 47, 49, 50, 51, 55, 56, 59, 60, 61
pervert, 14
phone, 8, 31, 37, 42, 43, 54, 58
prayer, 2, 7, 10, 15, 19, 23, 29, 35, 44, 47, 50, 52, 55, 56, 58, 59, 60
prayer line, 50
praying, 1, 58, 59
preaching, 1, 48
pregnant, 3, 5, 18
premature labor, 6
pretty, 5, 16, 49, 58
pride, 34
prison, 24, 42
production company, 54, 55
prophesied, 2
Prophet, 1, 39
Prophetess, 2, 34, 48, 49, 50, 51
Prophetess K, 2, 51

Index

Prophetess Kimberly Hargraves, 48
prostitution, 6

R

relationship, 9, 13, 17, 23, 26
relationships, 13
relatives, 8
rendezvous, 9
repenting, 2
residual hurts, 1
resignation, 33

S

San Bernardino, 28
Savior, 12
scholarship, 40
school, 3, 11, 12, 16, 19, 20, 21, 28, 29, 40, 45
School of the Prophets, 51
sex, 5, 9, 18
Shirley, 3, 16, 21, 24, 25, 26, 28, 31, 32, 34, 35, 36, 37, 39, 41, 48, 49, 50, 51, 59, 60
siblings, 4, 5, 9, 11, 12, 13, 14, 18, 24, 25, 36, 37, 38
sick, 24, 36, 37

sin, 11
singers, 13
sister, 3, 4, 5, 9, 14, 17, 28, 31, 33, 36, 37, 38, 39, 40, 41, 42, 43, 44, 46, 48, 49, 50, 54, 55, 57, 59, 60
son, 38, 61
Southern California, 3, 17, 50
sports, 40
STD, 22
Stephanie, 40, 44
storm, 2
Storm, 1
strange, 18
suffered, 6, 13, 16, 28
summer, 9
Sunday, 1, 12, 32, 33
supportive, 32
survive, 2, 3
swim meets, 9
swimming, 28

T

Tabatha, 41, 42, 43, 44, 59, 60
tacos, 38
teacher, 3, 12, 29

Index

temper, 8
testimony service, 56
Texarkana, 3
tithes, 17, 31, 34
town, 4, 11, 18, 25, 35, 38
traffic, 28
transcripts, 1
transparency, 2
Tron Moses, 2
truth, 16, 49, 55
Tuberculosis, 3

U

uncomfortable, 2, 50, 57, 58
unforgiveness, 23
unpaid tickets, 23

V

ventilator, 40
victim mentality, 51
Vodka, 4
vote, 32

W

warfare, 1
waters, 36
wheelchair, 24
wife, 30, 31, 32, 33, 34, 37
window, 9
witchcraft, 6
woman, 4, 14, 22, 59

Y

YouTube channel, 48

www.ingramcontent.com/pod-product-compliance
Lightning Source LLC
Chambersburg PA
CBHW071508070526
44578CB00001B/479